The Future of Classical Music

Part 1

First Edition

David Taylor

DEDICATION

To those questioning the status quo

CONTENTS

WHY THIS BOOK EXISTS

It's safe to say the classical music industry has had a rough few years. The COVID-19 pandemic halted performances and interrupted every part of our daily lives. This shock to the system made us adapt, discover new ways of doing things, learn new skills, and find any way to keep the music playing and our organisations running.

Over 2 years later, many people and organisations in the classical music world are now trying to "get back to normal" and return to the old way they used to do things.

For them, this shock to the system was just a temporary blip in extraordinary circumstances and it's now time to go back to business as usual. But for some, they began to question the whole system.

Why are audiences shrinking? Why haven't we made the most of digital opportunities? What is the concert going experience in the modern world? Is there a better way of doing things?

I've been talking and writing about the classical music world and the need for change for years. At first, it seemed like a hugely controversial topic, and it was hard to find other people on the same journey of exploring what the future of the classical music industry might look like.

As the pandemic hit, I saw a growing appetite to explore new ideas, question the status quo, and wonder what this future may look like. One of the benefits of the explosion of video meetings was the ability to speak to others on similar journeys, share experiences, and explore these new ideas.

One common theme from my conversations was that many challenging the status quo and exploring new ideas were usually in the minority in their organisations, and in some cases totally isolated.

As we enter the post-pandemic world, we are now seeing that many challenges we face were not as a result of the pandemic. Audiences are still down despite them returning in droves in other sectors, and we're still struggling to get on board with a digital world.

All of the issues we face now were there well before the pandemic. But what the pandemic has done is shine a light on them, and act as a rallying cry for the curious to start exploring and discussing new ways of doing things. For us to survive, the classical music industry needs to start having conversations about what the future looks like and how we get there.

This book exists to be a starting point for those conversations.

It's a collection of my articles, talks, and ideas from the last few years. They all have a common theme of finding a new way of doing things and tangible examples from other industries to act as inspiration.

It's designed to be flicked through, read in any order, used for reference, or consumed cover to cover.

It's meant to challenge the status quo and provoke conversations. For you to doodle on, share the ideas with others, try things out, and pass it on.

Also, as this is all about conversation and debate, you are definitely encouraged to disagree with things, have a dialogue as to why, and try different things out!

If you are one of the curious who feels like they are in the minority or isolated, I would love this to be an opportunity for you to find a community to explore new ideas with. The digital world has helped me find my community, with colleagues and even friends all over the globe and I would love it to be the same for you too.

Share your ideas and thoughts on this book or the classical music world in general with *#thefutureofclassicalmusic* on your social media platform of choice. Or, just check it out and see what other people are saying and thinking, and if you feel comfortable start a conversation with them. If in doubt, feel free to reach out to me and say hello as a starting point.

As the challenges we face continue to grow and change, we will need new ideas and answers (which is also why this book is just "part 1"). But we will also need people like you. It takes curiosity to question things, inspiration to create new ideas, and courage to challenge the status quo.

We're all in this together, and I'm excited to be exploring what the future of classical music may look like with you.

David Taylor

August 17th, 2022

www.david-taylor.org

1 - THE WORLD HAS CHANGED... AND SO MUST WE

This is my opening provocation from the digital session at the Association of British Orchestras conference in February 2022. It seemed like the perfect place to start...

2020 saw orchestras adapt faster than at any time during our history. Within the space of weeks, we saw orchestras learn new skills, adopt new ideas, and create digital content on a scale never seen before. Even though orchestras across the world were at totally different starting points in their digital journey, those journeys were equally difficult for all.

We should take huge pride in the effort that orchestras went to in order to keep music playing and making a difference to the lives of others, and it's important for us to both celebrate and understand our successes. This is something we will be looking at during today's session.

However, that was 2020. 2021 was very different and we now find ourselves beginning of 2022.

For the majority, digital has now either returned to being an afterthought or has in some cases completely stopped. Many have decided to "return to normal" and not have to worry about the additional burden of engaging with digital, even though it is clearly an integral part of the society we live in. We also have the additional challenge of the digital marketplace returning to normal after lockdown, and the competition with other highly effective digital content for people's attention is now greater.

The charity that audiences showed with our output in 2020 is no longer there and as a result, we've seen the inevitable decrease in engagement, ticket sales, and subscriptions for digital performances.

No longer can we create content that isn't suitable for the digital world or that doesn't conform to customer behaviour online and expect it to succeed like it did during the pandemic.

If we're being honest, our rapid expansion of digital in 2020 was not innovation... it was playing catch up. We both were and are far behind the world when it comes to digital.

It is telling that despite the digital age being the biggest change in how we communicate as a society since the invention of the printing press in the 1440s, and that digital has been the main way that we have connected to our audiences over the last two years, that this is the only session on digital at this conference.

If we were early adopters, the digital topics we would be covering at this conference would be about "how can orchestras balance the potential of NFTs with the environmental impact they have", "how could orchestras engage with the metaverse?", and "what can we learn from sports teams like Barcelona launching their own cryptocurrency".

However, we are not the early adopters. Despite the fact social media platforms have been around for years, with Instagram being 12, Twitter 16, YouTube 17, and Facebook 18, we as a sector still need to look at what makes good digital content, how we use social media, and even in some cases if we use it at all.

To reinforce how slow we are to adopt digital, we are having these conversations now when Facebook was launched way back in 2004... the same year Toxic by Britney Spears was top of the charts, Shrek 2 was the biggest selling film, and it is so long ago that Arsenal won the Premier League that year.

As well as showing how far behind we are, the pandemic also highlighted the digital illiteracy of classical musicians at all stages of their careers, with it being more significant for those with full-time orchestra positions. It is vital that going forward we do more to support and empower them with the skills and ways of thinking to be able to do what is now required of them in their roles, as well as to thrive in the world we live in.

The problems we face are less about digital itself, and more about how we adopt innovation in general. We are the laggards, trailing far behind the innovators and early adopters, hindered by outdated thinking and a systemic resistance to change. And this is largely because we are all trying to play an infinite game with a finite mindset.

A quick introduction to Game Theory. There are two types of games, finite and infinite. In a finite game there are known players, fixed rules, and an agreed upon objective that ends after a fixed period of time. Football is a finite game. In an infinite game there are both known and unknown players, there are no rules, and the only objective is to perpetuate the game. Business is in an infinite game, but businesses struggle or fail when they have a finite mindset.

The video rental company Blockbuster had a finite mindset. Despite having near total market domination, they refused to change and adapt with the times because they were stuck in a finite mindset and only worked within their finite rules. "A video rental company gives people a movie for a set period of time, and if they are late returning it, they are charged late fees".

When the small start-up Netflix moved to a subscription service, Blockbuster refused to do the same as it would mean giving up their previous way of thinking and doing things, where late fees made up 15% of their revenue. Long story short, because Blockbuster stuck to their finite mindset there is only one store left in the world which is run as a novelty Airbnb.

Companies with a finite mindset will have temporary success before they get to a point where they fail and will be surpassed by a player with an infinite mindset who more often than not is an unknown player.

So, at the start of 2022 we find ourselves at a fork in the road.

One path looks comfortable and familiar. We don't have to challenge the way we think or operate, and we can go back to playing our finite game. It leads us back to where we were before the pandemic, going through the motions, hoping the world doesn't change and that our audience will engage with us on our terms indefinitely.

Ultimately, this leads to us not keeping up with society and going the way of other organisations that have been too rigid to adapt to the world they operate in, like Blockbuster, like Skype, and like HMV.

The other path looks uncomfortable and unknown. It leads us through challenges, requiring us to reflect on ourselves and our previous ways of thinking, and begin to adopt an infinite mindset. It entails continual learning and development, embracing a culture of curiosity and change.

It also leads forwards, finding new opportunities, meeting our audience where they are in the world we live in, embracing digital, and developing the skills and ways of thinking to be able to constantly thrive in the future.

In short, the world has changed... and so must we

2 - ORCHESTRAS, YOUNG PEOPLE DON'T CARE ABOUT CHEAP TICKETS

A few years ago, I was on an industry panel thing at a music college alongside the CEO of an orchestra. One of the questions from a student to this CEO was *"when I come to your concerts, I rarely see any other young people. What are you doing to attract young people to your concerts?"*

Straight away, the CEO replied with an answer that could be copied and pasted by any other orchestra or concert hall in the world straight into their funding applications.

"We're actually doing lots to try and bring in young people to our concerts. We have a great under-30s scheme to provide discounted tickets to make sure concerts are as accessible to young people as possible".

Here's the thing. Cheap ticket schemes for young people do not work. Three big questions to answer then:

1. **Why do we think they work and why does everyone do them?**

2. **Why don't they work?**

3. **What could work instead?**

(Also, the term "young people" is exceptionally broad and one I usually don't like to use, but being all encompassing I'm going to keep using it for this blog)

So, why do we think they work and why does everyone do them? Many of you reading this may know of examples, articles, or even work in organisations where "under 30s schemes" etc have had a bump in ticket sales for young people. Although many will put this down to making tickets cheaper, this is in fact a "false positive".

These schemes are usually the only time that orchestras and venues will communicate with young people in a way that speaks to them. On top of that, they're usually accompanied by a huge marketing push. Take Wigmore Hall's under 35's scheme in partnership with Classic FM for example. Is the success of this scheme because tickets are only £5, or is it because they partnered with the largest classical music radio station in the UK who also have one of the largest social media followings of any UK radio station to promote attendance?

On top of this, those schemes are only a temporary fix. As soon as the cost goes up again, none of the underlying issues that have put young people off coming to concerts have been fixed and attendance drops again.

If the success of these schemes came down to cost being the barrier to making concerts accessible to young people, we'd expect to see queues into concerts like Black Friday, with halls being packed. This simply isn't the case. The increased communication and marketing push create a false positive that the scheme has worked.

The only reason the whole industry does these schemes is because it's all we've ever known. They're simple, unimaginative, and don't take much effort. More importantly, the bump we get from the false positive is enough to make us feel good that we've done something to improve things and it gives us something we can write on our funding applications. Conventional wisdom only leads to conventional results... and 99% of classical music organisations think conventionally.

Cheap ticket schemes don't work. The reasons behind this are more varied than that blanket statement suggests. For example, although the cost is now accessible, the environment often is not.

However, the reason I want to focus on is the one if find most interesting... cost is NOT a limiting factor for young people.

Let's take a Saturday concert and what could be on offer for you to do with your hard-earned cash as a young person in London...

- £5.00– classical music concert
- £5.10 – 1 pint of Stella in a Wetherspoons
- £5.29 – McDonalds medium size meal
- £9.99 – Vue cinema
- £13.50 – Crazy golf
- £16.99 – Dominoes takeaway medium pizza
- £26.50 – London Zoo
- £80.00 – Premier League football match

And this is all before we look at staying in options like Netflix or that the cost of new Xbox games now is £60 and upwards. Cost isn't the limiting factor for purchasing decisions that we think it and it is rarely the driver of the purchasing decision.

Young people are not looking for value for money... they are looking for value for time.

There are now so many demands on people's time of all ages. All people, but especially those 16-35 are now looking to get the most out of their time which involves maximising their experience.

Way back in 2016, the Association of British Orchestras conference had a fascinating session on "Behavioural Economics" by Rory Sutherland, Vice Chairman of the Ogilvy group (its founder David Ogilvy is often referred to as the "Father of Advertising"). As this is 6 years ago, I'm definitely going to misremember this story, but this one example has always stood out for me...

Customers were complaining that the Eurostar was too slow. There was a plan to spend, let's say, £10 million to upgrade the track so the train could go faster and make the journey 30 minutes shorter. But this was in fact looking at the problem incorrectly. The problem wasn't the length of the journey, it was the experience and customers were bored.

So instead of spending £10 million to make the train go faster, you could spend £1 million to install free WIFI and people wouldn't mind the length of the journey. Or you could even spend £5 million to employ supermodels to hand out free champagne and customers would want the train to go slower!

Orchestras are looking at the problem of "why aren't young people attending concerts" incorrectly. If instead of making tickets cheaper, they added value to the experience this would not only would this be more successful in attracting them to a concert, but young people may in fact pay more.

So, what could work instead of young person schemes and what could "adding value" look like?

There's so much potential for what this could look like and it's something where your imagination can run wild. But I think I've boiled it down to 5 different areas.

Community, shareability, products, services, and entertainment.

As someone who loves rugby, England games at Twickenham stadium are a great example of what this looks like for a different industry. In the compound outside the stadium, there's live music, ex-international players coaching junior tag rugby, a champagne tent, street food, and rugby skill tests for you to try your hand at. Inside the stadium there are restaurants, bars, and live social media interaction on screens going around the whole stadium where your posts can be shown. At the end of the day, people still put the performance on a stage by elite players first, there's just a lot more value for time.

So, some simple and actionable suggestions for classical music:

- Under 35s get a free drink with their tickets (probably cheaper than discounting tickets too!)

- Partnering with restaurants for dinner and concert deals

- Pre-concert instrument play area, where you can try an instrument for the first time

- Social media calls to action to allow relationships to continue after the event

- Box deals for groups of friends

- Post-concert meet the players

- Young professionals networking event

- Pre-concert speed dating.

- Red carpet area and other Instagram spots for social media photos (more on this in chapter 4)

3 - SEASON LAUNCHES ARE BORING...
BUT THEY DON'T HAVE TO BE

You know that time of year. Orchestras, opera houses, venues, and concert seasons are all launching their seasons for next year. And yet despite what should be the most exciting and interesting thing these organisations announce all year, I'm struck with just how boring, formulaic, and unoriginal they all are.

After chatting about this on Twitter and the frustrations of seeing the same boring tropes as the last 20 years, it got me thinking... is there a better way to launch a season and if so, what would it look like?

In this blog we're going to be looking at 4 things:

1. What makes season launches so boring?

2. Where can we look for inspiration for doing things differently?

3. What can we learn from this inspiration?

4. What a different approach to season launch could look like?

So, what makes season launches so boring and bland? As most audience members can't attend launch events and the pandemic has seen them get abandoned by most organisations, so announcing the season online has become more important than ever.

And yet 99% of season announcements use the same format. It's like all organisations get to this time of the year, open up the same shared template they've all been using for the last 20 years, copy and paste, and then fill in the blanks. Does this look familiar?

"We're really excited to announce our [insert year] season!

Priority booking is now available to our Friends. Find out how you can become a friend on our website

Browse our season here: [link]

General sale opens on [insert date]

[use a really boring slide show video that lists some concerts – text only, no talking]"

This format fails to say anything about why it's exciting, there isn't a clear voice or brand, it doesn't show the musicians or why they're excited, it totally fails to include the audience, and you certainly don't feel anything after seeing it. What should be the most exciting announcement of the year turns into a really bland piece of content with an ineffectual and pointless call to action to get people to sign up to the friend scheme. It creates zero buzz and is easy to ignore.

The vast majority of classical music organisations across the world do this year after year, so I was spoilt for choice when finding examples. But I've decided to show two of my favourite orchestras, the London Philharmonic Orchestra and the Philharmonia Orchestra, because they share some similarities that create challenges for them, and this shows the need for doing things differently.

Both the London Philharmonic Orchestra and the Philharmonia Orchestra announced their season on the same day at exactly the same time, they're based in the same city, they're both resident orchestras at the same venue (the Southbank Centre), and they have similar-ish names that have caused confusion in the past. With these challenges, it's really important for them to have clear and distinct season announcements. So, how did they do it?

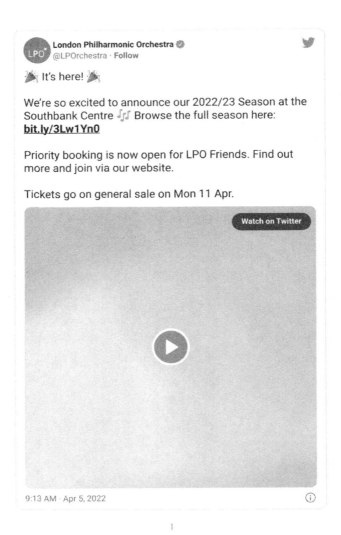

London Philharmonic Orchestra ✓
@LPOrchestra · **Follow**

🎉 It's here! 🎉

We're so excited to announce our 2022/23 Season at the Southbank Centre 🎵 Browse the full season here: **bit.ly/3Lw1Yn0**

Priority booking is now open for LPO Friends. Find out more and join via our website.

Tickets go on general sale on Mon 11 Apr.

Watch on Twitter

9:13 AM · Apr 5, 2022 ⓘ

1

---

[1] https://twitter.com/LPOrchestra/status/151127091292194406 9?s=20&t=uD94sSQEjaU-irBQxe4now

Philharmonia Orchestra ✓
@philharmonia · Follow

We're excited to announce the first half of our 22/23 London Season!
Priority booking is available now for Friends of the Philharmonia.

Have a look at the amazing concerts we have coming your way: **philharmonia.co.uk/seasons/2022-2...**

9:01 AM · Apr 5, 2022

2

[2] https://twitter.com/philharmonia/status/1511267703461498881?s=20&t=nawgUsh9Vakn93TlUuyWUQ

You'd be forgiven for thinking that these announcements were written by the same person.

Are you excited after seeing this? Do you feel a connection? Do you think they're different in any way?

Both lack a clear voice to distinguish themselves from each other, any sense of what makes it exciting or unique, anything about the musicians, a graphic that brings any value, and you certainly don't feel anything after reading it.

With this flawed approach being the industry norm, is there somewhere we can look for inspiration?

The Tech world is reliant on creating buzz around product launches to generate sales. Before the pandemic, product launches were large in-person events, inviting journalists, industry leaders, and the public to attend and try out the latest gear. The pandemic has caused this to permanently change, moving to online and creating large scale digital announcement events to launch their products. This approach means they can now reach a global audience.

There are plenty of examples of great launch events, like Samsung and Huawei, but there is one company that is a mile ahead of the rest that can act as a great inspiration for classical music organisations... Apple.

Since the pandemic began, the Apple Event has become gigantic. It dominates social media trends in the run-up, the event itself, and the weeks afterwards. The way the event is set up and created significantly helps to generate buzz, build connections, tell a story, and communicate a clear identity.

The Apple Event now happens multiple times a year, and if you fancy taking a look yourself, you can have a quick peek on YouTube.

If you don't have a spare 1 hour, here are my takeaways of what makes it amazing:

- Story first approach

- Putting the customer at the centre of the story

- Showing customers participating and using products to build connections

- Clear voice and identity

- Multiple presenters who all have different roles in the organisation, talking about their specialism – always a person, never the voice of the company

- Multiple locations, showing behind the scenes of the organisation

- Bringing in external industry users to talk about their experience to build connections

- Showing celebrities using the products

- Makes you feel something – shows how you would feel if you used their products

- Visually stunning

The majority of these takeaways focus on the audience/customer, putting them at the centre of the story and using people to build connections.

The result? A launch that is engaging and entertaining that builds strong connections with their audience and customers. Whether you like Apple or not, it's hard not to feel something after watching it.

It's also totally unique and clearly identifiable as Apple. If you tuned in halfway through, didn't know what you were watching, or see any of the products, you would know it was Apple in 10 seconds.

The success of Apple Events is much more than just the event itself. Apple are masters at building a sense of intrigue, drip-feeding small clues as to what's happening in the event. The team released teasers in advance that give the theme of the event. These teasers are always from individuals at Apple, and rarely the corporate account (again, always the voice of a person, never the corporation).

Greg Joswiak ✓
@gregjoz · Follow

We're California Streaming on September 14th. See you real soon. 🎵 **#AppleEvent**

Watch on Twitter

4:04 PM · Sep 7, 2021　　ⓘ

3

During the event itself, there are plenty of ways for audiences to engage. #AppleEvent dominates social media and this isn't by accident. On Twitter, each Apple Event has its own unique "hashflag" and animation for when you hit the like button, getting people engaging.

---

[3] *https://twitter.com/gregjoz/status/1435272731746979840?s=20&t=41TjgZJKmFdwGtoMOwxAew*

If it was all about the money, wouldn't Samsung and Huawei's events be just as good? What separates Apple is the thought that is put into the events. Revisiting my takeaways of the Apple Event and what makes it so good, most of them are totally free. In fact, the only ones where cost is a limiting factor are "visually", using "hashflags", and maybe "showing celebrities using products". Everything else is achievable with just a little thought and care.

So, what could this approach look like for a season launch?

First, move the launch to be a digital show, rather than just an announcement. This gives chance for anyone to attend, engage, and share. It also creates an opportunity to be totally creative with what is then produced.

Then, include musicians talking directly to the viewer. What excites them about the music and why do they think the audience would enjoy it? What do they hope the audience will get out of coming to the concerts? You can then hear from audience members themselves! Show them at concerts, talk to them about what makes coming so special and what they're excited for coming up. All of this is to make the viewer the protagonist in their own story and let them picture themselves at a concert.

Like Apple showing celebrities using products, then hear from the visiting musicians. And not a 10-second stock clip of them performing somewhere else, but a video message talking directly to the audience, building a connection before they come and perform. You can then have local figures and celebrities who love the music.

All of this can be done at multiple locations. Although I love this being behind the scenes of a concert hall, as most orchestras/opera houses/festivals are tied to a location, why not use this as a chance to get out and show the place! Local landmarks, and favourite spots of the musicians, all to connect the audience to you. You could even have a segment in location at an education project that the organisation runs.

In teasing the launch, have musicians, artists, and individuals tease the event and not just the company's Twitter account. Everyone in the organisation is in this together and individuals are able to build connections much more than companies.

During the event itself, encourage viewers to engage with the event, use a hashtag and empower them to share it. Then go a step further and have journalists and influencers engage in real time to share their views and spread the message even further through their networks.

For me, there is so much potential and so many creative ways to make season launches exciting. With such incredible music and fascinating musicians at the heart of it, they really don't have to be boring.

4 - CAN ORCHESTRAS FOLLOW ART MUSEUMS AND EMBRACE "INSTAGRAM TRAPS"?

The digital age, social media, and smartphones have changed so much of the world we live in and how we interact with it. This creates a particular challenge for all of us in the arts when people now want to interact and engage with art in a totally different way to what we're used to and the format we've created.

The temptation with all this change is to shy away from it, to only allow people to engage with art on our terms. But what if we were to embrace this change? Well, it turns out art museums already have...

I recently stumbled across a video by Vox called "How 'Instagram traps' are changing art museums[4]" and I'm totally fascinated by it and what it could mean for classical music.

It's well worth pausing reading this to find it on YouTube, but if you don't have chance to watch it right now here's a very quick summary...

"Instagram Traps"—installation art-ish environments built for social media—have become a serious cultural force with growing popularity. Popular examples include "The Museum of Ice Cream", "The Museum of Selfies",

---

[4] https://youtu.be/Qx_r-dP22Ps

and "The Museum of Feelings". This may all sound like a trendy fad, but they're already changing how we engage with art.

These interactive art pieces separated into themed rooms are incredibly popular right now, but the idea isn't new. It actually has its roots in "installation art" in the 1960s, when artists began to create 3d artwork designed for a specific space to be immersive and interactive. Yayoi Kusama's work is a great example of this, and is now being exhibited to take advantage of the Instagram age by traditional museums.

The explosive success of "Instagram trap" pop-ups has made traditional museums rethink how they do things. This usually begins with museums' photography policies. The Renwick Gallery started posting "photography encouraged signs" in 2015. About this change, Sara Synder of the Renwick Gallery says, "it was our way of saying, boldly: 'it's ok, you can be who you are, mediate your experience in the museum however feels right to you".

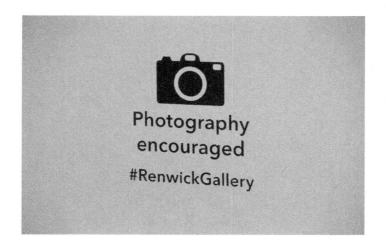

The impact of adopting this new digital and interactive approach is made greater when museums have taken a step further and hosted selfie-friendly shows. The exhibit "Wonder" helped break the Renwick Gallery's yearly attendance record in just six weeks[5]. When the Hirshorn held a 3-month show of Kusama's infinity mirrors, the museum increased its membership by a staggering 6,566%[6]!!!

So, that's the summary of the video, what can orchestras take from this?

The impact of embracing this approach is obviously huge. Which orchestra doesn't want to break its yearly attendance record in six weeks?! The question for orchestras isn't what the impact could be, it's more about "what do you do?" and "how do you do it?". For me, this can be broken down into three different areas:

---

[5]https://www.theatlantic.com/entertainment/archive/2016/02/instagram-art-wonder-renwick-rain-room/463173/
[6] https://news.artnet.com/art-world/yayoi-kusama-hirshhorn-museum-959951

- Changes to the traditional concert experience

- Producing specific interactive selfie-friendly performances

- Creating "Instagram traps" at concert venues that are outside the performance

First, let's look at making changes to the traditional concert experience. Art museums did something that was unthinkable 10 years ago in encouraging photography, and I think it's safe to say that encouraging this during orchestra concerts may feel the same. However, there are two levels of doing this, with one building on the other.

At a basic level, encouraging photography during performances allows audiences to capture their experience and share it on social media. In 2022 we're all used to the etiquette of turning phones on silent in concerts and cinemas etc. We're also now getting used to digital concert programme notes so using phones isn't totally new.

It's always a good thing to encourage good behaviour though, so adding welcoming text to urge audiences to take photos, but also turn phones on silent and more importantly their screen brightness down is an easy win to make sure those who take photos and those who don't all feel included. Then, adding a hashtag for people to use, interact with, and engage on.

Taking this up a level is having a live hashtag feed on a large screen above the orchestra during the concert. This definitely isn't something for during the performance, but having the opportunity to see your social media posts on a large screen during the interval and at the end of the concert is a strong driver to get people to interact and engage. Something you'll see on digital boards at any sports stadium. This is something I've helped deliver at multiple concerts on different continents, and as well as having the desired impact so far it has received zero complaints from audiences.

But I know for many that changes to the traditional concert going experience may be a step too far. Also, a limit of that idea is that "Instagram traps" are largely about putting the individual in the photo and selfies during these concerts would be pretty much impossible. So, what would another solution look like?

Taking inspiration from art museums in designing selfie-friendly installations, what about creating performances with audience engagement and photography in mind? A concert that totally changes the audience format to allow for movement and interaction, and also a setting that is visually appealing which will look great in photos. This experiential format is something we're already experimenting with in the sector, although I'm not sure how much the "Instagram trap" idea is considered in creating them.

My mind instantly went to concerts like *"The Sound Within"* by Southbank Sinfonia and *"Inside Beethoven"* by Aurora Orchestra, where musicians are scattered around the room and the audience can wander around inside the orchestra during the performance.

Events like this have the huge benefit of being able to create a bespoke experience where photography and selfies are encouraged, and they can be designed to be as photographic and Instagram friendly as possible. The potential of events like this is huge as it embraces the nature of what makes "Instagram traps" successful. The downside is that they are large-scale projects that can take a lot of effort to create which may be a barrier for some organisations.

So, is there a solution that wouldn't involve changing the traditional concert going experience or doing high-effort large-scale projects? If we think about the whole concert going experience being more than just the performance and the hall... yes.

The concert going experience starts well before the music starts, as audiences arrive outside the venue, go to a pre-concert talk, chat, go to the bar etc. So, why not use the time before the concert, during the interval, and after the concert for "Instagram traps"?

I saw some great examples of this at Dubai Opera, where outside the hall there was a large #DUBAIOPERA sculpture and an illuminated water feature. Then inside there was a red-carpet area for selfies and plenty of other gorgeous backdrops and areas for photos. An Instagram experience for the Instagram city. Ideas like this are easy to implement, cheap to do, and don't make any changes to the concert going experience.

We're already starting to see some in classical music lean embrace audience members using social media. The Royal Opera House are a great example of an organisation that meaningfully engages with audience members who share their experiences on social media and will often share their photos on ROH's social channels.

Even with concerns about how this changes the experience of concerts, the impact and potential of adopting this "Instagram trap" idea is obviously huge. The Vox video that inspired this blog ends with this:

"At the end of the day, even if social media is a big part of why so many people show up, they are showing up. And if this means more people engage with art they wouldn't have paid attention to otherwise, that feels pretty promising for the future of art."

If this is the case, isn't it about time orchestras embrace it?

5 - IN THE AGE OF THE CELEBRITY CEO, WHY ARE ORCHESTRA BOSSES INVISIBLE?

50 years ago, most people would not be able to name a single CEO of one of the world's biggest companies. Now, not only can most people name a long list of CEOs, but we're basically obsessed with them.

We live in the age of the celebrity CEO, where the founders and CEOs of companies have large public personas and their followings usually eclipse those of the organisations they run. Their journeys, ideas, and opinions are of great interest to people all over the world.

Think Steve Jobs, Bill Gates, Sheryl Sandberg, Elon Musk, Jeff Bezos, Susan Wojcicki, Richard Branson... the list goes on.

Even on a smaller business scale, the CEOs who are in Dragon's Den (or Shark Tank in the USA) don't run Fortune 500 companies, but they are all household names with large social media followings and appear on other TV shows.

These CEOs are the figureheads, ambassadors, and champions of their companies, the thought leaders of their industries and the world we live in. Being visible is of huge importance for raising the profile of their business and converting people to join their businesses' cause and share their values.

The world of orchestras couldn't be further away from this modern age of the celebrity CEO, with bosses being invisible to the public and even to those within the industry. It's rare to know who they are and rarer still to know what their values or thoughts on the industry are.

I recently attended the Association of British Orchestras conference which got me thinking about this as an idea. Those orchestra bosses at the conference that were a part of panels and sharing their thoughts on the future of the industry were in the minority.

Last year I wrote an article on "*10 classical music thought leaders you should really be following*" and as part of it asked for other people's suggestions on Twitter. Looking back, I didn't include a single orchestra boss on my list and I'm certain that they were absent from others' suggestions too.

I imagine that most musicians, students, and audiences won't know who the CEOs of professional orchestras are. Taking me out of my UK comfort zone, despite working in the nuts and bolts of the orchestra industry I can only name one CEO of orchestras in the USA.

A quick bit of research on the 14 full-time professional symphony orchestras in the UK* and their CEOs. Only 10 of those CEOs have a professional social media account. Only 3 have an account that you could describe as "regularly active". Only 1 has a following over 1,000. None are sharing their ideas or thoughts on the industry.

A fun challenge if you're reading this, name as many orchestra bosses in your country as you can. If you can, do you know what their thoughts on the industry are or what their values are?

You might be asking yourself "why is this important?". For me, there are two answers. It's of huge benefit for the orchestra they run and it's of vital importance to the future of orchestras and classical music as a whole.

Let's start with the first one. Why is it a huge benefit to the orchestras? The good news is that orchestra bosses are already the figureheads of their organisations. It's just not overt. CEOs regularly meet dignitaries, patrons, and sponsors. They host fundraising events, attend industry events, and network on their behalf.

This is the same for these celebrity CEOs. However, they take it a step further and have a widespread and global impact. The success of this stems from the fact that people build relationships and trust with individuals a lot easier than they do with faceless corporations. As a result, they can build a much larger following and convert people to join their cause a lot easier than their company.

For example, Elon Musk's 77.3m Twitter followers compared to Tesla's 1.5m. Richard Branson's 12.6m Twitter followers compared to Virgin's 250k. Jessica Alba's 19.5m followers on Instagram compared to The Honest Company's 1m... you get the picture.

The good work that orchestra bosses do behind closed doors could be hugely amplified by being visible and overt. Imagine what the fundraising, reputational, or ticketing potential could be if the orchestra boss were to build strong meaningful relationships at scale through digital, press, and media, sharing the story of the orchestra, its direction, and its cause with others!

It goes much further than this. By sharing their methodology, leadership style, and cause, they can attract others to work with them. Either by becoming a talent magnet for those wanting to join their cause and ultimately work with them and the orchestra, or by identifying potential partner organisations to collaborate with. The impact of having a visible leader building relationships at scale and sharing the cause of the orchestra could be huge and long-lasting.

For me, there is also strong a second reason for why we need our leaders in classical music to be visible. We are living through a period of unprecedented disruption. The consequences of the digital age, recovering from a global pandemic, climate change, and plenty more are felt throughout all walks of life.

For the classical music and orchestral industry, we are facing more challenges to justify our place in the world, either for the attention of our audience, funding from governments and trusts, or our purpose in society. These challenges are only going to get bigger, and it is short-sighted to think that we are not in for a serious fight for the future of orchestras in the next 10 years. We need vocal and visible leaders to not just be ambassadors of our industry and art form, but to become active champions of it, rolling up their sleeves and fighting for its future.

This is a situation where we are all very much in it together. Campaigning for the future of orchestras and classical music has a significant impact. This isn't just about looking out for an individual orchestra or those orchestras that get the big Arts Council funding grants. This is about justifying classical music's place in society to both decision-makers and to the public, which then impacts freelance musicians, teachers, amateur ensembles, education projects, music in care homes, children... all of us!

So, if there are so many benefits to being a visible leader and a strong case for why we need visible leaders for the industry, why are orchestra bosses invisible?

Looking at the bigger picture, the reasons for this are similar to the reasons behind many of the orchestral industries' challenges. As an industry, we really aren't good at adopting change. Whether this is digital, marketing, technology, HR, innovation etc. we tend to struggle. The role of the CEO in the modern world is different now than it was 20 years ago for all industries, and some have adapted faster than others. We need to start adopting this different idea of what the modern orchestra boss looks like to make it the expected norm within the industry and that this becomes part of their job role.

Now, the smaller picture is a little more complex. CEOs are human. And being human, there are a whole range of thoughts, feelings, and anxieties. There are likely to be lots of reasons on a personal and individual level that stop CEOs from being visible and vocal champions. Many will have to adopt new ways other thinking and doing things to be able to do this. Being an "influencer", or rather a "person of influence", in the modern is a skill. It takes work, but it is something that can be learnt and fits into the strengths and passions of the individual.

Orchestra bosses should be taking the initiative themselves to start being visible and learning about how to become visible and a "person of influence" in the modern world to champion their orchestras and classical music. But we also need to support and empower them. I think there could be a lot that we as an industry could do to help with this, whether that is through organisations like the Association of British Orchestras and League of

American Orchestras to facilitate training, the orchestras themselves finding CPD opportunities for our leaders, or indeed all of us rallying round to support them. After all, we are all in this together.

*UK full-time symphony orchestras – LPO, LSO, RPO, Philharmonia, Halle, RLPO, CBSO, BSO, RSNO, Ulster Orchestra, BBC SO, BBC Philharmonic, BBC NoW, BBC SSO

6 - WHY THE BBC PROMS IS THE SKYPE OF CLASSICAL MUSIC - AND WHY IT'S IN CRISIS

For years, Skype had almost total market dominance. If you wanted to video call someone, you were going to use Skype. By the time a small competitor called Zoom was founded in 2011, Skype had used its 8-year head start to grow to over 100 million users. Hell, it had even become so big that in the same year *The Onion* joked[7] that "Skype" would be added to the dictionary and three years later, the verb was added to the Oxford English Dictionary. You know you've made it when you've become a verb.

All that Skype needed for world domination was for more people to use video calls as part of their daily life. And yet 18 months after a pandemic forced the whole world online and to use video calls for all elements of our lives, the end of July will see "Skype for Business" being discontinued, with Skype's market share down to 6.6%.

Skype's lack of competition during its period of dominance led to complacency, stagnation, and pointless and poorly rolled-out updates. When the world went online and Skype realised that it was no longer the

---

[7] *https://www.theonion.com/oxford-english-dictionary-to-add-skype-and-coat-to-late-1819572447*

only gig in town and that it was behind the pack, it was too late to do anything. What should have been the period for the company's ultimate success was its time of crisis and demise.

As well as seeing the discontinuation of Skype for Business, the end of July sees the start of this year's BBC Proms, another organisation that for years (in fact decades) has seen near total market dominance and now is facing a similar crisis.

For context, this blog isn't going to be about the music. It's not even going to be about attending concerts. This is going to be about the broadcast coverage of the BBC Proms and both how and why it's facing a crisis that it hasn't recognised yet.

For years in the UK, if you wanted to see an orchestra on the TV you had to watch the Proms. The only other concerts that might be televised that year would be BBC Young Musician of the Year, the Vienna Philharmonic New Year's Day concert, the odd documentary, and the odd one-off. The Proms however would be around 30 televised concerts all over a couple of months in summer, with the whole festival being broadcast on the radio. Let's face it, watching an orchestra on TV was watching the Proms.

Like Skype, this dominance has led to complacency, stagnation, and a mediocre product. The coverage of the Proms has both looked and felt the same for years. If you've got a few minutes, have a look on YouTube for clips of the BBC Proms from both 2012 and 2022.

Ignoring the poor YouTube quality, there are no changes in how they are filmed, and neither are cinematically or visually appealing (bonus points if you noticed that they're still using the same fonts in the titles). If we're being honest from a cinematography/broadcast perspective, they look a bit naff and it's a mediocre product. On top of that, I can't think of another BBC programme that looks identical 10 years apart.

Then around the filming, the coverage, and presenting have stayed the same since I started watching as a child. The same predictable presenter line-up each year, shot in the same way from the same box in the Royal Albert Hall, with the same dull segments and same dull interviews of artists that bring little to either excite or give any real insight. Again, think of other BBC programmes like Match of the Day and how radically they've changed their format, included technology, and created other supporting content both on TV and social media.

Speaking of, then there is the world of social media. I've been frustrated for years at how appalling the Proms' use of social media is and how it's a huge missed opportunity for them. The ability to share stories, music, and connect to people across the country and around the world should be at the heart of what the Proms is and with such an incredible product should be an easy job.

And yet social media is used in such a clichéd corporate fashion to remind us that tickets are on sale and that we can order Proms guides, that it would be an outdated approach 10 years ago. This is no surprise though with BBC Radio 3's refusal to engage meaningfully with social media leading it to last year use its only Instagram post since 2014 to tell us that it's not using Instagram – ignoring a platform with over 1.2 billion users. But again, this is a stark contrast compared with BBC Sport's and Radio 1's excellent use of social media, especially with live music events like Glastonbury and Radio 1's Big Weekend.

So where did all this leave the Proms leading into the pandemic? The Proms has openly said it wants to connect to more people and increase viewership for years. As everyone went online or to their TVs during lockdown, surely this would be the perfect time to reach more people in a meaningful way, especially for the world's largest music festival backed up by the world's largest broadcasting company? It turns out, it was in a very similar position to Skype.

Before the pandemic, we started to see the rise of competitors such as Medici TV and Marquee TV who were filming, purchasing, and broadcasting performances. We also had Sky Arts move to be free in the UK offering an alternative place for arts and culture content on TV. Then we also had the odd organisation broadcasting their own performances, such as the Royal Opera House, New World Symphony, and the Berlin Philharmonic. Finally, we have the world of social media, with YouTube being home to some amazing performances for years and Classic FM's excellent reach on multiple channels.

Then the pandemic begins, and orchestras start to react by moving online and broadcasting their own content. What is so striking by this is that they haven't been limited by any previous way of doing things, so what we see is a ton of filmed concerts that not only sound just as good as the Proms, but they LOOK SO MUCH BETTER. But don't just take my word for it...

The Philharmonia Orchestra, Queensland Symphony Orchestra, and LA Phil are 3 great examples of orchestras creating some stunning video content that are worth stopping reading and looking up. It's ok, put the book down and have a look... I'll wait.

There's almost no comparison to the as they're leagues apart. You certainly wouldn't think that out of these it's the Proms is the video that's backed up by the largest broadcasting company in the world. And these were just 3 examples, with plenty of other options from LPO, LSO, OAE, Scottish Opera, and more.

And then there's the supporting content that has been done around these concerts. Bournemouth Symphony Orchestra and the Liverpool Philharmonic are some great examples of the success orchestras had at hosting pre-concert zoom rooms and breaking down the barrier between audience and musician (something the Proms didn't do in 2020). The RSNO smashed it out of the park by adding a ton of social media projects around their concert season, with educational challenges, interviews, smaller performances, and instrument guides. RNCM threw the rule book out the window and started their own live presenting format for concerts, pulling musicians off stage in between pieces to chat and encouraging genuine engagement from the audience that was watching, and then responding directly to them during the broadcast in a meaningful way. This ended up with a presenting format that is so much more engaging than what we've seen elsewhere.

The Proms has now gone from pretty much the only place to watch an orchestra at home to not even being in the top 10 in the space of 18 months. This is then compounded by a total lack of any signs of change. So where does that leave the Proms, why does it need to change, and what can it do? All can be explained by "Game Theory".

Anyone who has heard me speak this year knows that I've become a little obsessed with Game Theory and Simon Sinek's book "The Infinite Game"[8], and how they

[8] https://simonsinek.com/product/the-infinite-game/

apply to our sector. This could be a whole blog in itself, so here is a very brief run through

There are two types of games, finite and infinite. In a finite game there are known players, fixed rules, and an agreed upon objective that ends after a fixed period of time. Football is a finite game. In an infinite game there are both known and unknown players, there are no rules, and the only objective is to perpetuate the game. Business is an infinite game, and businesses struggle or fail when they have a finite mindset.

The video rental company Blockbuster had a finite mindset. Despite having near total market domination, they refused to change and adapt with the times because they were stuck in a finite mindset and only worked within their finite rules. "A video rental company gives people a movie for a set period of time, and if they are late returning it, they are charged late fees". When the small start-up Netflix moved to a subscription service, Blockbuster refused to do the same as it would mean giving up their previous way of thinking and doing things where their late fees made up 15% of their revenue. Long story short, because Blockbuster stuck to their finite mindset there is only one store left in the world which is run as a novelty Airbnb.

Companies with a finite mindset will have temporary success before they get to a point where they fail and will be surpassed by a player with an infinite mindset who more often than not is an unknown player. For example, record stores globally have struggled, with HMV in the UK falling into administration numerous times as they had a finite mindset, and their business model was disrupted not by another music company but by someone totally unknown... a tech company called Apple who led the music streaming revolution and the market away from physical records. If they had an infinite mindset of "bringing music to as many people as possible" instead of the finite mindset of "sell as many records as possible" they wouldn't have failed.

The Proms has had a finite mindset for decades. It has done the same thing in the same way each year, playing by the same rules, and measuring its success in the same way. Each year the same old template is rolled out of the cupboard, and everything goes on autopilot. When it has been worried by competition it has been from other "known players", like what else is on TV at the same time, Sky Arts, maybe things like Medici TV. Two years ago, if I'd said that every orchestra around the world would be filming and distributing their own digital performances no one would have believed it (I certainly wouldn't have). But here we are, and the Proms now has hundreds of "unknown players" across the world putting out a better product with an infinite mindset in a way that is relevant and meaningful to people in the time we live in.

The Proms may not be in an overt crisis this year, but the crisis point is definitely now if it wants to stop its future demise. If it were to carry on the same path it would follow in the same footsteps as Skype, Blockbuster, and HMV. It wouldn't be a question of if it would fail, but when.

I know that "Proms bashing" happens every year (see any article about the Last Night of the Proms 2020) and that it's so easy to criticise things when you don't suggest a solution – something that drives me nuts. I adore the Proms, the reason I'm in the music world is from seeing a cello on the Proms as a child, and the only way for me to really see orchestras growing up in part of the UK miles away from an orchestra was to watch the Proms. So, after a lot of hard truths, here's my solution to save the future of the Proms.

Switch to an infinite mindset. OK, yes that's the answer, but how does that work? Well, fortunately, the Proms has already figured this out for me...

"The aim of the BBC Proms is to bring the best in classical music to the widest possible audience, which remains true to founder-conductor Henry Wood's original vision in 1895."

– The BBC Proms website[9]

This aim is an infinite mindset! To prove it, just think back to how this applied in the past. When innovations in radio and TV happened, they weren't ignored as the Proms stuck to in-person concerts, they were embraced

---

[9]*https://www.bbc.co.uk/programmes/articles/2kSNxH9Cj9PT62 ZzTnvWpYZ/the-bbc-proms-whats-it-all-about*

to create a series that reached millions of people not just in the U.K. but across the world.

That ethos at its core can apply to anything the future throws at the Proms. The internet and social media age, augmented reality, VR, humans living in space... you can see it working whatever the future throws at it.

So, what in reality needs to happen is that the Proms needs to go back to its roots and start putting its aim into practice. There needs to be a long pragmatic look as to whether they really have been working to "bring the best in classical music to the widest possible audience" or whether they've just been going through the motions with the same thinking and the same mediocre product for the last 10 years. On top of that, taking a look at what their product is and evaluating where it lines up alongside its competitors.

The Proms needs to take inspiration from all the lessons, mistakes, and successes of the rest of the orchestral world over the last 18 months. From there, it needs to start upping the quality of filmed products to catch up, devising better content ideas for supporting content, and making a significant move into the digital and social media world.

The good news is that for working out how to do this, the Proms can look for help and support from elsewhere within the BBC. The "how" of doing social media for a music festival could surely be sorted out by talking with BBC Radio 1 about how they have 7.5 million subscribers on YouTube and what do they do for Radio 1's Big Weekend, or BBC Sport about creating supporting content around live events. There has to be some help and support on improving the filmed quality of the Proms by talking to the BBC team behind the incredibly cinematic Blue Planet or the beautifully filmed

"Secrets of the Museum" at the V&A. There really is so much potential for the Proms here.

There is plenty of hope that the proms won't go the way of Skype and Blockbuster, but it needs to go back to its roots and start putting its aim into action.

7 - OF COURSE ORCHESTRAS CAN MAKE MONEY ONLINE... HERE'S HOW

From writing about classical music going online quite a lot now I've noticed a theme being repeated over and over again which is really bugging me, and it sounds something like this:

"orchestras can't make money online"

I'm here to tell you... that's nonsense. Of course orchestras can make money online.

Well, I'm actually here to tell you why we perceive that orchestras can't make money online, and what orchestras can do to generate income from their digital output. But... you know... that isn't a great title.

So why do we perceive that orchestras can't make money online?

It's actually a relatively simple answer. We're attempting to measure the success of digital output through a 20th century direct and transactional system, rather than a 21st century indirect system that's based on values, connections, and relationships.

Considering I just made most of those terms up as I was writing them, let's unpack what I actually mean.

The vast majority of classical music organisations largely run their performance-related income on the idea that "there will be a thing", "people will want the thing", "people pay money to have the thing". In this case, "the thing" is the performance or an event.

This has been the case for the last century, and all of us in the classical music world have worked on this model that our audience are there to pay money straight away and pay it directly up front to see us. And... IT WORKED.

Success is measured in the terms of "will people pay to see us" and "how many people will pay to see us".

In terms of making money online, this doesn't really cut it. Just look at your own experiences. Do you pay money upfront to watch anything on YouTube? Or on Facebook? Or hosted on someone's website? I sure as hell don't.

Also, why would I pay say £5 to watch a single concert online on one day, when ALL of Disney Plus is £5.99 for a month and ALL of Netflix is £5.99 for a month? Paying to watch a concert online doesn't provide comparable value in terms of both cost and time.

And yet, we're STILL trying to measure our success in the same we measured live concerts. On top of that, we're trying to get to the point of charging for our content as soon as possible. Yes, we've put some free concerts online for a bit, but we're now going to charge for them.

For example, The Royal Opera House has been livestreaming previous recordings and will now be doing reduced live performances, but after the first show they will charge £4.99 to watch the others. Now, I totally empathise with this as we're all rightly worried about money, which ROH has been transparent about, but in the long term isn't going to be as effective.

To use a ridiculous analogy, receiving money from audiences online is like dating. If you go on your first date and while you're waiting for the starter to arrive you go in for a snog, you're probably going to get a slap and they'll leave. But, if you invest time, care, and attention, maybe show random acts of kindness, and even take an interest in the things they like over a long period you might end up with a spouse.

To use a more tangible analogy for the orchestra world, we should treat our online audience like big potential donors. Take time to understand who they are, make them feel valued, and then finally ask them for money.

If you want to know more about this sort of approach, the book "Jab Jab Jab Right Hook" by Gary Vaynerchuk[10] is incredible.

_____

[10] *https://www.garyvaynerchuk.com/books/*

So, if the old ways aren't going to work, how do we change to an "indirect system that's based on values, connections, and relationships"... and WTF is that David.

Welcome to the exciting bit...

How orchestras can make money online

The good news is people are making money online from loads of things, so we can just use their model. Regardless of the genre, everyone makes money online using the same basic setup.

1. Generate attention with content that provides value to an audience

2. Use that attention and value to build strong connections and meaningful relationships

3. Monetise those strong connections and meaningful relationships through multiple income streams and advocacy that also provide value.

Simple right?

Well if it was easy, everyone would be doing it. It's hard work. Think about it though, so is learning an instrument. It doesn't happen overnight.

I'm going to break down how this works, and then run through a non-musical example, and an orchestra example.

1 - Generate attention with content that provides value to an audience

Things are kind of crowded online at the moment as... you know... everyone is online. But it doesn't mean you can't create content that generates attention and provides value.

Also, I wanted to dispel a myth about attention online. You 100% should aim to be the biggest in your world. Notice the word "your" instead of "the".

You don't need a gazillion followers, or likes, or views, but you do need to aim at being the biggest in your world that you operate in. Yes, being online means you have a global audience, but using it to connect well to as many people in your world has way more benefits. This can be a world in terms of both geography or niche.

With the content, it also needs to provide value. Although spamming content to get noticed as much as possible gets results, it's working out how you can provide value to your audience that will have the most benefits for stage 2. Spamming content isn't about frequency but more about the type of content. For example, if your orchestra posts 20 times a week saying tickets are on sale (don't worry, we've all done it) isn't going to work for you.

2 - Use that attention and value to build strong connections and meaningful relationships

Once you start to provide value you can start to build relationships. This is done in the same way as a friendship. By continually providing things that are of value, and by taking an interest and connecting to build relationships.

The first is easier to do at scale as you continue to put out the same amount of content whether you have 100 followers or 1 million.

Taking an interest and connecting to build relationships... this is going to take some legwork. Some of this can be including your audience, asking for feedback, and finding opportunities to interact. The hardest parts will be directly communicating with individuals and offering individual acts of kindness.

3 - Monetise those strong connections and meaningful relationships through multiple income streams and advocacy that also provide value

The fun bit! How do you actually make money? Well, if you see any YouTubers etc, direct advertising on their videos only makes up for a small amount of income. So in order to make money, they have multiple income streams.

There are two categories for this, and both monetise the connection and relationship you have with your audience

A – *from your audience*

This is in essence asking for money from your audience. Donations can be a feature, especially on Twitch, but the vast majority are offering a product or service in return for money. For example, products that provide value for your audience, online courses, merchandise, the list is endless. Anything that you can think that your audience would want and gives them something of value that they would part money for.

B – through advocacy – "Be a George"

Mini story time. I have a friend called George. Over the time I've known him, we've spoken about films, music, TV, life, everything. On top of that, I know about George's strengths and expertise.

The result is, I listen to George. So when a film comes out and the reviews are bad but George says that I'll like it I go to the cinema. When he sends me a recommendation of a band I'll drop what I'm doing to listen to them. When he suggests a microphone I'll buy it without doing any other research because I trust his expertise. When he advocates something I don't just listen, I act, and I buy.

In the online world, you need to "Be a George" for your audience. Getting to that point of trust where your audience sees their thoughts, values, and tastes aligned with yours. From here, you can be an advocate.

Fun fact, you can REALLY monetise advocacy. Whether this is offering sponsorships in your content, brand affiliations, or amazon affiliate links, there are plenty of opportunities to generate income based on your ability to advocate other companies' products and services

Now that's all the theory blurb out of the way, let's run through a non-musical example, then what an orchestra could do.

Non-musical example – Peter McKinnon

Peter McKinnon is a Canadian photographer and YouTuber who makes videos on photography and filmmaking. He is also one of my favourite YouTubers.

I've watched him and his content constantly for a few years, as he puts out high-quality content of great value that he doesn't charge for.

1. He regularly uploads videos, sometimes multiple times a week. Either tutorials, Q&A, travel videos, interviews, or entertainment, but something that always gives value

2. He connects with his audience. There will be regular collaborative photography or filmmaking projects where the audience gets involved, and he then showcases what others have made. There are also requests for tutorial topics and Q&As. On top of that, he spends a ton of time talking to people in the comments

3a. He provides products and services that his audience wants or needs. He has a range of digital download packs so you can colour grade your photos like him, sound effects, and graphics. He also now has a range of camera gear including his own specialist backpack and lens filters. And then he also has a range of coffee (he's big into coffee), hats, and other merchandise.

3b. Then there's the advocacy. He regularly talks about the equipment he uses and provides affiliate links to buy them. Then there are product reviews with affiliate links as well. On top of that, there are brand affiliations with Canon, Squarespace, Skillshare, and Epidemic Sound. And finally, sometimes he will travel and make a video which is sponsored.

So, what is the impact? As a Yorkshireman, I pride myself on refusing to take my wallet out of my pocket unless I have to. And yet I own every single digital download he's sold. Pretty much the sole reason all my equipment is Canon is because of watching his videos. I changed to iPhone after a video he made reviewing the camera. There pretty much isn't a camera-related purchase I've made where I haven't consulted his opinion.

I've repeatedly spent large amounts of money on either his products or things that he has recommended. And those recommendations are things that as a creator he's been able to monetise.

What an orchestra could do

Right, so how can this work for an orchestra?

1. Put up digital video content at scale - performances, individual recitals, educational content, entertainment, interviews - as much as possible that provides value to your audience

2. Include the audience in musical challenges, masterclasses, Q&A's. Reach out to your audience, involve them, highlight what they're doing and get them to be a part of a community

3a. Provide products or services that the audience needs – so anything you can think of, both musical and non-musical. Musical being things like lessons, masterclasses, workshops, education projects, recordings, digital downloads, and even equipment and instruments. Who would want to use the LPO's strings or have a Berlin Phil reed? Non-musical being merchandise and hospitality-related experiences.

3b. Endorsement time. There is big money in instrument and equipment sales. So partnering with strings companies, instrument cases, brass mutes etc. It doesn't have to be garish "THIS IS SPONSORED BY YAMAHA" content. If you always see LA Phil use Larsen strings then you'll probably want a set.

Think about children around the world buying Cristiano Ronaldo's football (soccer) boots, or Venus William's tennis racket... or the marketing phenomenon Air Jordans. Basically, the world's top athletes and sports showcase Nike, then position orchestras to do the same for music-related brands.

If you don't have the partnerships, use affiliate links to monetise anything that you recommend that can be purchased.

Then there's the non-musical advocacy. In a rare bit of praise for the Vienna Philharmonic Orchestra being forward-thinking, they always talk about what the orchestra are wearing for the New Year's concert. So why not pair with designers to showcase fashion? Then reverse engineering what most classical music audiences like to find other potential sponsors. What wine does the orchestra drink on tour, what watches do they wear to keep time, how do they keep fit, what cars do they drive, what newspapers do they read, which department store do they shop at, what glasses do they wear. Literally, the possibilities are endless when you start to think about brand synergy and what sort of companies and marketers would like to reach the audiences that orchestras have.

These are all ideas off the top of my head with little thought too. There is SO much potential and room for exploration and experimentation here.

I know that this is a bit of a culture shift. I really do. But we really need to start thinking differently in order to generate income for orchestras, and doing so online is going to have benefits right now when we can't perform live, and later to add to our revenue streams when we do. Like playing an instrument, making money online is hard to do, and had to do well instantly. But there are obviously rewards out there.

As a final note, these are the five highest earners on YouTube in 2019[11]:

1.   Ryan Kaji - $26 million
2.   Dude Perfect - $20 million
3.   Anastasia Radzinskaya - $18 million
4.   Rhett and Link - $17.5 million
5.   Jeffree Star - $17 million

---

[11] https://www.cnbc.com/2019/12/20/ryan-kaji-remains-youtubes-highest-earner-making-26-million-in-2019.html

Wouldn't it be great to see an orchestra up there in the next decade?

8 - CLASSICAL MUSIC AUDIENCES ARE VANISHING... WHY AREN'T WE DOING ANYTHING ABOUT IT?

As the 2021/2022 seasons come to an end, we reach a moment of realisation. Classical music audiences are vanishing... and they're not coming back.

From talking to organisations and musicians across all levels of the industry, in-person audiences are down around 30%. My own experience of attending concerts certainly echoes this, with one well established classical event I went to having around 50% attendance, with one of the performances only having 38 people in the audience!

This is also backed up by a recent study by WolfBrown and the League of American Orchestras[12] that found the 26% of pre-covid concert attendees have said they're not ready to resume live performances, and that we're looking at 15%-20% long term non-returners. I imagine many non-returners won't be taking the time to fill out surveys about something they're not going to, so this figure is likely to be higher.

Surely this significant drop is due to the pandemic? Sadly, this is not true. That same WolfBrown study found that less than half of non-returners cite health concerns as

---

[12] https://www.audienceoutlookmonitor.com/post/june-27-executive-briefing-with-alan-brown-goodbye-again-hello-uncertainty

a reason for not returning. What is most striking though is looking at how other industries are coping in 2022 after the pandemic. Average Premier League attendance was higher in the 2021/22 season than the pre-pandemic season of 2018/2019[13], and Glastonbury 2022 had its highest ticket sales for 15 years[14].

Anyone who has travelled recently can testify that human behaviour is very much in a post-pandemic phase. Packed trains, buses, and planes, with no spacing and few masks... this is a very different world to 2020.

The reality is that the significant and industry wide drop in classical music attendance is not due to COVID. We are now seeing the consequences of decades of systemic resistance to change, a stagnant and unevolved product, and unoriginal and out-of-date marketing.

---

[13] https://sportsgazette.co.uk/2021-2022-football-attendances/
[14] https://en.wikipedia.org/wiki/Glastonbury_Festival#2020s

So, what now? For a second, we'll take the classical music out of this. Any business that faced a 30% drop in annual sales would be in crisis. The panic button would be hit, extraordinary meetings called, and the board would be demanding change. For a business in this situation there are three options available if they didn't want to fail.

1. Adapt how the product is marketed

2. Adapt the product

3. Both 1 and 2

Doing absolutely nothing and just repeating what has been done before isn't an option for an organisation that wants to still exist. Can you imagine Apple suffering a 30% drop in sales and doing absolutely nothing? Or Nike? Or Manchester United? Or Amazon? Or Tesco?

Or Disney? No! That would be insane, and we would think they are insane.

So, what are organisations doing in the classical music industry in the face of a 30% drop in audiences? Nothing... and this is insane.

As I've already written about in chapter 3, orchestras not only are launching next year's seasons in the same dull boring way as they always have, but they're doing it the same as each other. As well as failing to capitalise on the incredible potential of digital and doubling down on outdated marketing strategies, at times they're failing to even get the basics of social media right.

There is also little evidence that the "product" of classical music has changed. In chapter 2, I wrote about how we should be offering value for time and not value for money to attract young audiences, but that concept and idea of adding value to the concert experience as a whole is vital to audiences of any age. The "regular" concert experience has been largely untouched for over 100 years, and with audiences vanishing it's obviously not working.

With the need for change screaming at us in the face, we should look at how other organisations have dealt with having to make radical changes in the face of ruin.

There are plenty of examples we could look at. Marvel comics went from financial crisis to global phenomenon by switching its focus from paper comics to cinema. One of the most famous examples of a company that has repeatedly tried to reinvent itself is Nintendo. Originally a playing card company, they had some failed experiments at switching products (including instant rice, "love hotels", and a taxi service), before becoming a toy company in the 1960s, and then a video game company in the 1970s. But in this blog, we'll be looking at a business that has had similar struggles to the classical music industry and adapted both its product and how it was marketed... Formula 1.

In 2016, Formula 1 had a problem. The glamour of the last 70 years was wearing off and 2010 and 2015 Formula 1 global fan surveys revealed significant dissatisfaction in the fan base. It was failing to attract younger audiences, the presentation of Formula 1 hadn't changed in decades, it had failed to embrace digital, and despite several attempts, Formula 1 had never managed to crack the American market. The number of people tuning in to watch fell from 600 million in 2008 to about 400 million in 2015 (a fall of about 30%... sound familiar?)

Despite being credited with the rise in popularity of Formula 1 in the 1970s, their CEO Bernie Ecclestone was now drastically out of touch with the modern world. In one interview he famously said:

"I'm not interested in tweeting, Facebook and whatever this nonsense is. I'd rather get to the 70-year-old guy who's got plenty of cash. So, there's no point trying to reach these kids because they won't buy any of the products here and if marketers are aiming at this audience, then maybe they should advertise with Disney."[15]

You wouldn't be surprised if this quote came from an orchestra in 2022.

It was clear Formula 1 was not in the 21st century. Fortunately, in late 2016 it was bought out by Liberty Media who made an instant change... they changed

---

[15] *https://www.reuters.com/article/us-motor-racing-ecclestone-idUSKCN0IY19S20141114*

Formula 1 from a motorsports company to a media company.

Two years later, the cornerstone of this new approach launched. The Netflix series "Drive to Survive" was a whole new take on Formula 1 and an instant success, becoming one of the most watched shows on Netflix. Part docuseries, part operatic drama, it focuses on behind-the-scenes action and driver/team rivalries as much as on-track racing. In fact, only about 20% of Drive to Survive is actual racing and the presentation is totally different from what you have seen before for Formula 1.

The show has also allowed important current issues to be a part of the Formula 1 discussion. For example, the driver Lewis Hamilton's stand on racial injustice, We Race As One to acknowledge the global fight against COVID, and the commitment to have a net-zero carbon footprint by 2030. In the modern world, values matter as much as the product, and F1 is embracing this.

Another big change was that all fans were given equal importance and the chance to interact with the sport. There is a difference between a customer and a fan, and that is passion. Liberty Media understands that passion, especially in sports, ultimately drives sales.

Previously, drivers were not allowed to be on social media. Hamilton joked that Bernie sent him cease-and-desist letters whenever he posted clips on Instagram. Drivers were now encouraged to be on social media, where Hamilton now has 29.4 million Instagram followers. The entire sport is now focused on this with teams flourishing online and race content focused on engaging fans. Restrictive TV deals which were the cornerstone of Formula 1's success in the 1970s were loosened so clips could be shared on social media. If you look back at the trailer for season 4, it opens with a montage of tweets from viewers, a statement of intent about social media's place in the sport.

So, what was the result? Last year saw an estimated increase of 73 million fans globally, 77% of that growth was driven by the 16-35 demographic, and a 40% increase in viewership in the USA[16]. Oh, and its valuation increased from $8 billion to $13 billion in just 3 years. From radically adapting both the product and how it was marketed, Formula 1 went from an existential crisis and inevitable oblivion to a thriving success.

One of the reasons I choose to focus on Formula 1, rather than an example like Nintendo, is that in adapting its product it didn't reinvent the wheel. Whereas what Nintendo does now is totally different to what it did in the

---

[16] https://www.theguardian.com/media/2021/dec/17/netflixs-drive-to-survive-americans-f1-fans

1950s, Formula 1 is still about fast cars going around a track lots of times. This is why it should serve as such inspiration for the classical music industry.

Classical music can stay at its core about classical music, it doesn't need to reinvent the wheel. Performances should still have this right at the heart of what we do. But the "product" of what we do is so much more than the notes that come from an instrument. Like Formula 1 changing from being a motorsports company, all of us in classical music should change to be a "media and in-person entertainment company".

The concert experience starts well before the first note is played, and this is where we need to start experimenting and adapting with what our in-person product is. Like Formula 1, we have not embraced digital and social media despite the central role it plays in society and the benefits of embracing it being so painfully obvious.

In chapter 1 I argued the case for immediate change. As a quick reminder, here's my closing statement from it.

"So, at the start of 2022 we find ourselves at a fork in the road.

One path looks comfortable and familiar. We don't have to challenge the way we think or operate, and we can go back to playing our finite game. It leads us back to where we were before the pandemic, going through the motions, hoping the world doesn't change and that our audience will engage with us on our terms indefinitely.

Ultimately, this leads to us not keeping up with society and going the way of other organisations that have been too rigid to adapt to the world they operate in, like Blockbuster, like Skype, and like HMV.

The other path looks uncomfortable and unknown. It leads us through challenges, requiring us to reflect on ourselves and our previous ways of thinking, and begin to adopt an infinite mindset. It entails continual learning and development, embracing a culture of curiosity and change.

It also leads forwards, finding new opportunities, meeting our audience where they are in the world we live in, embracing digital, and developing the skills and ways of thinking to be able to constantly thrive in the future.

In short, the world has changed... and so must we"

6 months later and the case for change is greater than ever. We have more and more data saying that we're in trouble and we know audiences are vanishing. In many ways, the crisis classical music is facing is like the climate emergency. The evidence that we need to change has been there for years and is growing daily, crisis events happen to hit us in the face and remind us of the need for immediate change, and yet we refuse to take the action we need to guarantee our own survival.

With these blogs I try to have a constructive approach, giving examples from other industries about alternative approaches that can act as inspiration for change. It's something I'm going to continue to do, but there comes a point where we need to get out of the clouds and take action.

We can't wait for another programming cycle to do something, or to see how this season goes.

We need to act, and we need to act now.

9 - ORCHESTRAS ARE LOOKING FOR ANSWERS IN THE WRONG PLACES

I was chatting with an orchestra about ways they could attract new audiences and become more accessible. The orchestra's concert dress was very traditional, full white tie and tails for the men, so I suggested that like other orchestras they should switch to something just as smart but less elitist and outdated.

"Oh, we actually thought about doing that, so we did a survey of our audience to ask them what we should do. They told us they like the tails, so we didn't change".

Asking the audience might seem like the logical thing to do in a situation like this. When it comes to making decisions, most orchestras ask their audience for feedback. Although this comes with the best of intentions, they're actually looking for answers in the wrong places... and that's because of "survivorship bias".

In World War 2, the US air force were wanting to minimise the loss of bombers by adding armour to the planes. As planes need to be light enough to fly, there's a limited amount of armour they could add, so to make sure they were putting armour in the right places the air force started to do some research.

When bombers returned from a mission, the air force logged the location of all the damage on the plane. It looked something like this:

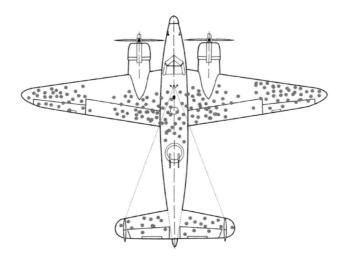

For the air force, the data was conclusive and the way forward was clear. They wanted to add armour where the planes were being shot, the areas where all the dots are. It's very logical to think the same thing looking at the diagram. If you're going to put more armour on the plane, you'd put it on the areas where the data says they're being shot.

Fortunately, the air force had statistician Abraham Wald working on the project. He spotted that their analysis was missing a valuable part of the picture, the planes that were hit but that hadn't made it back.

All those planes that returned to base and had their damage logged were the survivors. The bullet holes they were looking at actually indicated the areas a plane could be hit and keep flying – exactly the areas that didn't need reinforcing.

Wald suggested that the air force should do the opposite of putting armour where the data said planes were being shot, and put it in the places they weren't (all those white sections without dots). The result was that more planes came back safely.

Effective decision making requires a detailed look at data, but it's very easy not to see the whole picture. In classical music we're obsessed with audience data, but in many circumstances we're not asking the right people.

The big crisis classical music is now facing is why audiences are continuing to fall in the post-pandemic world when other industries have bounced back.

The question we are now asking is "how can we attract more people to concerts?". But if we think about survivorship bias, why are we asking our existing audience and making decisions based on their answers?

In chapter 8 I argue that the core reason behind the drop in audiences is that for decades we haven't adapted our product or how it's marketed with the times.

Our existing audience are the survivors. They are the survivors of our bad product, they are the survivors of our bad marketing, and to bring this blog full circle, in some cases they are the survivors of our elitist and outdated concert dress.

If we want to improve things, we can't make decisions based on the answers of the survivors. We might even have to make decisions that go against them.

One of my guilty pleasures is Kitchen Nightmares with Gordon Ramsey. If you've not seen it, Gordon goes into a terrible restaurant and helps the owners turn it around... usually with lots of shouting as the owners rarely want to change and shouting is kind of Gordon's thing. Every restaurant is so bad that all the solutions are painfully obvious, so you as the viewer get frustrated at how ridiculously bad they are but also get to feel smart that you come to the same solution as a world-famous chef.

Anyway, the reason I bring this up is one exchange between Gordon and the owner of one of these failing restaurants. The owner started arguing with Gordon as he was worried that *"the existing customers are going hate the changes"*, to which Gordon replied, *"and how many people is that?"*.

In being aware of the survivorship bias in our audience research, we may have to make decisions that are not only different to what our existing audience want, but may be the opposite. The audience for the orchestra at the beginning of the blog may not only prefer the orchestra preferring tails, but they may actually hate any change in concert dress. But with audiences diminishing, Gordon would say *"and how many people is that?"*

If we are going to bring new audiences to concerts and survive, we're going to have to start doing some things that feel counterintuitive. We have to look for answers in the right places.

ABOUT THE AUTHOR

Described as an "arts innovator" by the BBC, David Taylor is an entrepreneur, consultant, coach, and speaker who helps people and organisations in the classical music industry thrive in the modern world. In 2018 he was named on the Forbes 30 under 30 list.

www.david-taylor.org

#thefutureofclassicalmusic

Printed in Great Britain
by Amazon

26577857R00076